LEARN YOUR

Here are some of the essential f
will be using depending or

Palomar Kn(

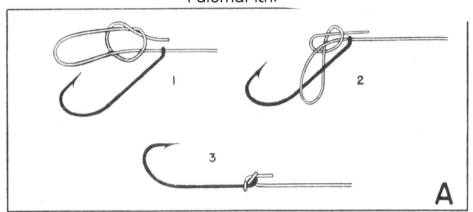

1

2

3

A

Davy Knot

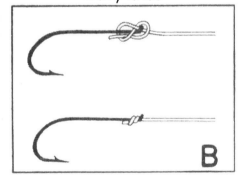

B

Double Fisherman's Knot

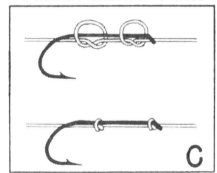

C

Multi-Hook Knot

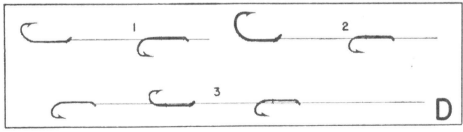

1

2

3

D

Remember to always have an adult nearby when tying your fishing line, hooks are very sharp and can poke you!

ALL ABOUT LURES & BAITS

LURES vs. BAITS

Whether you use lures or baits will depend on the species of fish you are trying to catch, and the water conditions. The fish will not be nearly as active when the water temperature is cold, and when the temperature is warm, sometimes there will be a frenzy!

Cold Water
Smelly &
Inactive Bait

Normal Water
Live Bait &
Soft Lures

Warm Water
Swim Baits
& Jigs

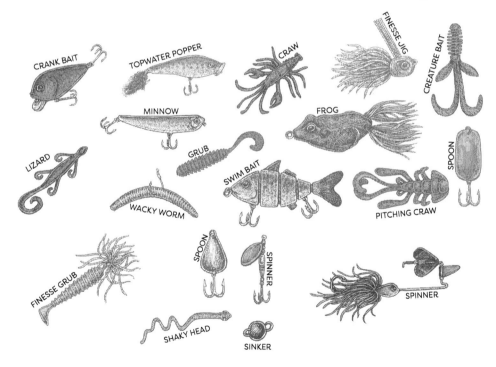

FISH TO LOOK OUT FOR

Largemouth Bass
Water Type:
Rivers & Lakes
Preferred Lure:
Worms, Craws & Cranks
Max Weight:
22 lbs 5 oz
☐
I've Caught One!

Smallmouth Bass
Water Type:
Rivers & Lakes
Preferred Lure:
Blades, Tubes & Grubs
Max Weight:
11 lbs 15 oz
☐
I've Caught One!

Pink Salmon
Water Type:
Ocean, Rivers & Great Lakes
Preferred Lure/Bait:
Salmon Eggs & Jiggs
Max Weight:
13 lbs 10.6 oz
☐
I've Caught One!

Bluegill
Water Type:
Rivers & Lakes
Preferred Lure/Bait:
Crickets & Worms
Max Weight:
3 lbs 15 oz
☐
I've Caught One!

Crappie
Water Type:
Rivers & Lakes
Preferred Lure:
Minnows, Worms & Insects
Max Weight:
5 lbs 4.6 oz
☐
I've Caught One!

Fishing Log

Location:_____ Date:_____
Location Details: _____
_____
Companions:_____
Water Temp:_____ Air Temp:_____
Hours Fished:_____ Wind Direction:_____
WInd Speed:_____ Humidity:_____

Weather ☀ ⚡ _____
Moon Phase:_____
Tide Phase:_____
Notes:_____

Species:	Bait:	Length:	Weight:	Time:
Other Notes:				
Other Notes:				
Other Notes:				
Other Notes:				

Fishing Log

Location:_____ Date:_____
Location Details: _____
_____
Companions:_____
Water Temp:_____ Air Temp:_____
Hours Fished:_____ Wind Direction:_____
WInd Speed:_____ Humidity:_____

Weather ☀⚡ _____
Moon Phase:_____
Tide Phase:_____
Notes:_____

Species:	Bait:	Length:	Weight:	Time:
Other Notes:				
Other Notes:				
Other Notes:				
Other Notes:				

Fishing Log

Location:_____ Date:_____
Location Details: _____
_____
Companions:_____
Water Temp:_____ Air Temp:_____
Hours Fished:_____ Wind Direction:_____
WInd Speed:_____ Humidity:_____

Weather ☀️⚡ _____
Moon Phase:_____
Tide Phase:_____
Notes:_____

Species:	Bait:	Length:	Weight:	Time:
Other Notes:				
Other Notes:				
Other Notes:				
Other Notes:				

Fishing Log

Location:_____ Date:_____
Location Details: _____
_____
Companions:_____
Water Temp:_____ Air Temp:_____
Hours Fished:_____ Wind Direction:_____
WInd Speed:_____ Humidity:_____

Weather ☼ ⚡ _____
Moon Phase:_____
Tide Phase:_____
Notes:_____

Species:	Bait:	Length:	Weight:	Time:
Other Notes:				
Other Notes:				
Other Notes:				
Other Notes:				

Fishing Log

Location:_____ Date:_____
Location Details: _____
_____
Companions:_____
Water Temp:_____ Air Temp:_____
Hours Fished:_____ Wind Direction:_____
WInd Speed:_____ Humidity:_____

Weather ☀ ⚡ _____
Moon Phase:_____
Tide Phase:_____
Notes:_____

Species:	Bait:	Length:	Weight:	Time:
Other Notes:				
Other Notes:				
Other Notes:				
Other Notes:				

Fishing Log

Location:_____ Date:_____
Location Details: _____
_____
Companions:_____
Water Temp:_____ Air Temp:_____
Hours Fished:_____ Wind Direction:_____
WInd Speed:_____ Humidity:_____

Weather ☀ ⚡ _____
Moon Phase:_____
Tide Phase:_____
Notes:_____

Species:	Bait:	Length:	Weight:	Time:

Other Notes:

Other Notes:

Other Notes:

Other Notes:

Fishing Log

Location:_____ Date:_____
Location Details: _____
_____
Companions:_____
Water Temp:_____ Air Temp:_____
Hours Fished:_____ Wind Direction:_____
WInd Speed:_____ Humidity:_____

Weather ☀ ⚡ _____
Moon Phase:_____
Tide Phase:_____
Notes:_____

Species:	Bait:	Length:	Weight:	Time:
Other Notes:				
Other Notes:				
Other Notes:				
Other Notes:				

Fishing Log

Location:_____ Date:_____
Location Details: _____
_____
Companions:_____
Water Temp:_____ Air Temp:_____
Hours Fished:_____ Wind Direction:_____
WInd Speed:_____ Humidity:_____

Weather ☀⚡ _____
Moon Phase:_____
Tide Phase:_____
Notes:_____

Species:	Bait:	Length:	Weight:	Time:

Other Notes:

Other Notes:

Other Notes:

Other Notes:

Fishing Log

Location:_____ Date:_____
Location Details: _____
_____
Companions:_____
Water Temp:_____ Air Temp:_____
Hours Fished:_____ Wind Direction:_____
WInd Speed:_____ Humidity:_____

Weather ☀ ⚡ _____
Moon Phase:_____
Tide Phase:_____
Notes:_____

Species:	Bait:	Length:	Weight:	Time:
Other Notes:				
Other Notes:				
Other Notes:				
Other Notes:				

Fishing Log

Location:_____ Date:_____
Location Details: _____
_____
Companions:_____
Water Temp:_____ Air Temp:_____
Hours Fished:_____ Wind Direction:_____
WInd Speed:_____ Humidity:_____

Weather ☀⚡ _____
Moon Phase:_____
Tide Phase:_____
Notes:_____

Species:	Bait:	Length:	Weight:	Time:
Other Notes:				
Other Notes:				
Other Notes:				
Other Notes:				

Fishing Log

Location:_____ Date:_____
Location Details: _____
_____
Companions:_____
Water Temp:_____ Air Temp:_____
Hours Fished:_____ Wind Direction:_____
WInd Speed:_____ Humidity:_____

Weather ☀ ⚡ _____
Moon Phase:_____
Tide Phase:_____
Notes:_____

Species:	Bait:	Length:	Weight:	Time:
Other Notes:				
Other Notes:				
Other Notes:				
Other Notes:				

Fishing Log

Location:_____ Date:_____

Location Details: _____

_____

Companions:_____

Water Temp:_____ Air Temp:_____

Hours Fished:_____ Wind Direction:_____

WInd Speed:_____ Humidity:_____

Weather ☀⚡ _____

Moon Phase:_____

Tide Phase:_____

Notes:_____

Species:	Bait:	Length:	Weight:	Time:
Other Notes:				
Other Notes:				
Other Notes:				
Other Notes:				

Fishing Log

Location:_____ Date:_____
Location Details: _____
_____
Companions:_____
Water Temp:_____ Air Temp:_____
Hours Fished:_____ Wind Direction:_____
WInd Speed:_____ Humidity:_____

Weather ☀⚡ _____
Moon Phase:_____
Tide Phase:_____
Notes:_____

Species:	Bait:	Length:	Weight:	Time:
Other Notes:				
Other Notes:				
Other Notes:				
Other Notes:				

Fishing Log

Location:_____ Date:_____
Location Details: _____
_____
Companions:_____
Water Temp:_____ Air Temp:_____
Hours Fished:_____ Wind Direction:_____
WInd Speed:_____ Humidity:_____

Weather ☀⚡ _____
Moon Phase:_____
Tide Phase:_____
Notes:_____

Species:	Bait:	Length:	Weight:	Time:
Other Notes:				
Other Notes:				
Other Notes:				
Other Notes:				

Fishing Log

Location:_____ Date:_____
Location Details: _____
_____
Companions:_____
Water Temp:_____ Air Temp:_____
Hours Fished:_____ Wind Direction:_____
WInd Speed:_____ Humidity:_____

Weather ☀️⚡ _____
Moon Phase:_____
Tide Phase:_____
Notes:_____

Species:	Bait:	Length:	Weight:	Time:
Other Notes:				
Other Notes:				
Other Notes:				
Other Notes:				

Fishing Log

Location:_____ Date:_____
Location Details: _____
_____
Companions:_____
Water Temp:_____ Air Temp:_____
Hours Fished:_____ Wind Direction:_____
WInd Speed:_____ Humidity:_____

Weather ☼ ⚡ _____
Moon Phase:_____
Tide Phase:_____
Notes:_____

Species:	Bait:	Length:	Weight:	Time:
Other Notes:				
Other Notes:				
Other Notes:				
Other Notes:				

Fishing Log

Location:_____ Date:_____
Location Details: _____
_____
Companions:_____
Water Temp:_____ Air Temp:_____
Hours Fished:_____ Wind Direction:_____
Wind Speed:_____ Humidity:_____

Weather ☀ ⚡ _____
Moon Phase:_____
Tide Phase:_____
Notes:_____

Species:	Bait:	Length:	Weight:	Time:
Other Notes:				
Other Notes:				
Other Notes:				
Other Notes:				

Fishing Log

Location:_____ Date:_____
Location Details: _____
_____
Companions:_____
Water Temp:_____ Air Temp:_____
Hours Fished:_____ Wind Direction:_____
WInd Speed:_____ Humidity:_____

Weather ☀️⚡ _____
Moon Phase:_____
Tide Phase:_____
Notes:_____

Species:	Bait:	Length:	Weight:	Time:
Other Notes:				
Other Notes:				
Other Notes:				
Other Notes:				

Fishing Log

Location:_____ Date:_____
Location Details: _____
_____
Companions:_____
Water Temp:_____ Air Temp:_____
Hours Fished:_____ Wind Direction:_____
WInd Speed:_____ Humidity:_____

Weather ☼ ⚡ _____
Moon Phase:_____
Tide Phase:_____
Notes:_____

Species:	Bait:	Length:	Weight:	Time:
Other Notes:				
Other Notes:				
Other Notes:				
Other Notes:				

Fishing Log

Location:_____ Date:_____
Location Details: _____
_____
Companions:_____
Water Temp:_____ Air Temp:_____
Hours Fished:_____ Wind Direction:_____
WInd Speed:_____ Humidity:_____

Weather ☀⚡ _____
Moon Phase:_____
Tide Phase:_____
Notes:_____

Species:	Bait:	Length:	Weight:	Time:
Other Notes:				
Other Notes:				
Other Notes:				
Other Notes:				

Fishing Log

Location:_____ Date:_____
Location Details: _____
_____
Companions:_____
Water Temp:_____ Air Temp:_____
Hours Fished:_____ Wind Direction:_____
WInd Speed:_____ Humidity:_____

Weather ☀️⚡ _____
Moon Phase:_____
Tide Phase:_____
Notes:_____

Species:	Bait:	Length:	Weight:	Time:
Other Notes:				
Other Notes:				
Other Notes:				
Other Notes:				

Fishing Log

Location:_____ Date:_____
Location Details: _____
_____
Companions:_____
Water Temp:_____ Air Temp:_____
Hours Fished:_____ Wind Direction:_____
WInd Speed:_____ Humidity:_____

Weather ☀⚡ _____
Moon Phase:_____
Tide Phase:_____
Notes:_____

Species:	Bait:	Length:	Weight:	Time:
Other Notes:				
Other Notes:				
Other Notes:				
Other Notes:				

Fishing Log

Location:_____ Date:_____
Location Details: _____
_____
Companions:_____
Water Temp:_____ Air Temp:_____
Hours Fished:_____ Wind Direction:_____
WInd Speed:_____ Humidity:_____

Weather ☀⚡ _____
Moon Phase:_____
Tide Phase:_____
Notes:_____

Species:	Bait:	Length:	Weight:	Time:
Other Notes:				
Other Notes:				
Other Notes:				
Other Notes:				

Fishing Log

Location:_____ Date:_____

Location Details: _____

_____

Companions:_____

Water Temp:_____ Air Temp:_____

Hours Fished:_____ Wind Direction:_____

WInd Speed:_____ Humidity:_____

Weather ☀⚡ _____

Moon Phase:_____

Tide Phase:_____

Notes:_____

Species:	Bait:	Length:	Weight:	Time:

Other Notes:

Other Notes:

Other Notes:

Other Notes:

Fishing Log

Location:_____ Date:_____
Location Details: _____
_____
Companions:_____
Water Temp:_____ Air Temp:_____
Hours Fished:_____ Wind Direction:_____
Wind Speed:_____ Humidity:_____

Weather ☀⚡ _____
Moon Phase:_____
Tide Phase:_____
Notes:_____

Species:	Bait:	Length:	Weight:	Time:
Other Notes:				
Other Notes:				
Other Notes:				
Other Notes:				

Fishing Log

Location:_____ Date:_____
Location Details: _____
_____
Companions:_____
Water Temp:_____ Air Temp:_____
Hours Fished:_____ Wind Direction:_____
WInd Speed:_____ Humidity:_____

Weather ☀⚡_____
Moon Phase:_____
Tide Phase:_____
Notes:_____

Species:	Bait:	Length:	Weight:	Time:

Other Notes:

Other Notes:

Other Notes:

Other Notes:

Fishing Log

Location:_____ Date:_____
Location Details: _____
_____
Companions:_____
Water Temp:_____ Air Temp:_____
Hours Fished:_____ Wind Direction:_____
WInd Speed:_____ Humidity:_____

Weather ☀ ⚡ _____
Moon Phase:_____
Tide Phase:_____
Notes:_____

Species:	Bait:	Length:	Weight:	Time:
Other Notes:				
Other Notes:				
Other Notes:				
Other Notes:				

Fishing Log

Location:_____ Date:_____
Location Details: _____
_____
Companions:_____
Water Temp:_____ Air Temp:_____
Hours Fished:_____ Wind Direction:_____
Wind Speed:_____ Humidity:_____

Weather ☀⚡ _____
Moon Phase:_____
Tide Phase:_____
Notes:_____

Species:	Bait:	Length:	Weight:	Time:
Other Notes:				
Other Notes:				
Other Notes:				
Other Notes:				

Fishing Log

Location:_____ Date:_____
Location Details: _____
_____
Companions:_____
Water Temp:_____ Air Temp:_____
Hours Fished:_____ Wind Direction:_____
WInd Speed:_____ Humidity:_____

Weather ☀ ⚡ _____
Moon Phase:_____
Tide Phase:_____
Notes:_____

Species:	Bait:	Length:	Weight:	Time:
Other Notes:				
Other Notes:				
Other Notes:				
Other Notes:				

Fishing Log

Location:_____ Date:_____
Location Details: _____
_____
Companions:_____
Water Temp:_____ Air Temp:_____
Hours Fished:_____ Wind Direction:_____
WInd Speed:_____ Humidity:_____

Weather ☀⚡ _____
Moon Phase:_____
Tide Phase:_____
Notes:_____

Species:	Bait:	Length:	Weight:	Time:
Other Notes:				
Other Notes:				
Other Notes:				
Other Notes:				

Fishing Log

Location:_____ Date:_____
Location Details: _____
_____
Companions:_____
Water Temp:_____ Air Temp:_____
Hours Fished:_____ Wind Direction:_____
WInd Speed:_____ Humidity:_____

Weather ☀️⚡ _____
Moon Phase:_____
Tide Phase:_____
Notes:_____

Species:	Bait:	Length:	Weight:	Time:
Other Notes:				
Other Notes:				
Other Notes:				
Other Notes:				

Fishing Log

Location:_____ Date:_____
Location Details: _____
_____
Companions:_____
Water Temp:_____ Air Temp:_____
Hours Fished:_____ Wind Direction:_____
WInd Speed:_____ Humidity:_____

Weather ☼ ⚡ _____
Moon Phase:_____
Tide Phase:_____
Notes:_____

Species:	Bait:	Length:	Weight:	Time:

Other Notes:

Other Notes:

Other Notes:

Other Notes:

Fishing Log

Location:_____ Date:_____
Location Details: _____
_____

Companions:_____
Water Temp:_____ Air Temp:_____
Hours Fished:_____ Wind Direction:_____
WInd Speed:_____ Humidity:_____

Weather ☀ ⚡ _____
Moon Phase:_____
Tide Phase:_____
Notes:_____

Species:	Bait:	Length:	Weight:	Time:
Other Notes:				
Other Notes:				
Other Notes:				
Other Notes:				

Fishing Log

Location:_____ Date:_____
Location Details: _____
_____
Companions:_____
Water Temp:_____ Air Temp:_____
Hours Fished:_____ Wind Direction:_____
WInd Speed:_____ Humidity:_____

Weather ☼ ⚡ _____
Moon Phase:_____
Tide Phase:_____
Notes:_____

Species:	Bait:	Length:	Weight:	Time:
Other Notes:				
Other Notes:				
Other Notes:				
Other Notes:				

Fishing Log

Location:_____ Date:_____
Location Details: _____
_____
Companions:_____
Water Temp:_____ Air Temp:_____
Hours Fished:_____ Wind Direction:_____
WInd Speed:_____ Humidity:_____

Weather ☀⚡ _____
Moon Phase:_____
Tide Phase:_____
Notes:_____

Species:	Bait:	Length:	Weight:	Time:
Other Notes:				
Other Notes:				
Other Notes:				
Other Notes:				

Fishing Log

Location:_____ Date:_____
Location Details: _____

_____
Companions:_____
Water Temp:_____ Air Temp:_____
Hours Fished:_____ Wind Direction:_____
Wlnd Speed:_____ Humidity:_____

Weather ☀⚡ _____
Moon Phase:_____
Tide Phase:_____
Notes:_____

Species:	Bait:	Length:	Weight:	Time:
Other Notes:				
Other Notes:				
Other Notes:				
Other Notes:				

Fishing Log

Location:_____ Date:_____
Location Details: _____
_____
Companions:_____
Water Temp:_____ Air Temp:_____
Hours Fished:_____ Wind Direction:_____
WInd Speed:_____ Humidity:_____

Weather ☀⚡ _____
Moon Phase:_____
Tide Phase:_____
Notes:_____

Species:	Bait:	Length:	Weight:	Time:
Other Notes:				
Other Notes:				
Other Notes:				
Other Notes:				

Fishing Log

Location:_____ Date:_____
Location Details: _____
_____
Companions:_____
Water Temp:_____ Air Temp:_____
Hours Fished:_____ Wind Direction:_____
WInd Speed:_____ Humidity:_____

Weather ☀⚡ _____
Moon Phase:_____
Tide Phase:_____
Notes:_____

Species:	Bait:	Length:	Weight:	Time:

Other Notes:

Other Notes:

Other Notes:

Other Notes:

Fishing Log

Location:_____ Date:_____
Location Details: _____
_____
Companions:_____
Water Temp:_____ Air Temp:_____
Hours Fished:_____ Wind Direction:_____
WInd Speed:_____ Humidity:_____

Weather ☀️⚡ _____
Moon Phase:_____
Tide Phase:_____
Notes:_____

Species:	Bait:	Length:	Weight:	Time:
Other Notes:				
Other Notes:				
Other Notes:				
Other Notes:				

Fishing Log

Location:_____ Date:_____
Location Details: _____
_____
Companions:_____
Water Temp:_____ Air Temp:_____
Hours Fished:_____ Wind Direction:_____
WInd Speed:_____ Humidity:_____

Weather ☀ ⚡ _____
Moon Phase:_____
Tide Phase:_____
Notes:_____

Species:	Bait:	Length:	Weight:	Time:

Other Notes:

Other Notes:

Other Notes:

Other Notes:

Fishing Log

Location:_____ Date:_____
Location Details: _____
_____
Companions:_____
Water Temp:_____ Air Temp:_____
Hours Fished:_____ Wind Direction:_____
WInd Speed:_____ Humidity:_____

Weather ☀⚡ _____
Moon Phase:_____
Tide Phase:_____
Notes:_____

Species:	Bait:	Length:	Weight:	Time:
Other Notes:				
Other Notes:				
Other Notes:				
Other Notes:				

Fishing Log

Location:_____ Date:_____
Location Details: _____
_____
Companions:_____
Water Temp:_____ Air Temp:_____
Hours Fished:_____ Wind Direction:_____
WInd Speed:_____ Humidity:_____

Weather ☼ ⚡ _____
Moon Phase:_____
Tide Phase:_____
Notes:_____

Species:	Bait:	Length:	Weight:	Time:

Other Notes:

Other Notes:

Other Notes:

Other Notes:

Fishing Log

Location:_____ Date:_____
Location Details: _____
_____
Companions:_____
Water Temp:_____ Air Temp:_____
Hours Fished:_____ Wind Direction:_____
WInd Speed:_____ Humidity:_____

Weather ☀ ⚡ _____
Moon Phase:_____
Tide Phase:_____
Notes:_____

Species:	Bait:	Length:	Weight:	Time:
Other Notes:				
Other Notes:				
Other Notes:				
Other Notes:				

Fishing Log

Location:_____ Date:_____
Location Details: _____
_____
Companions:_____
Water Temp:_____ Air Temp:_____
Hours Fished:_____ Wind Direction:_____
WInd Speed:_____ Humidity:_____

Weather ☀️⚡ _____
Moon Phase:_____
Tide Phase:_____
Notes:_____

Species:	Bait:	Length:	Weight:	Time:

Other Notes:

Other Notes:

Other Notes:

Other Notes:

Fishing Log

Location:_____ Date:_____
Location Details: _____
_____
Companions:_____
Water Temp:_____ Air Temp:_____
Hours Fished:_____ Wind Direction:_____
WInd Speed:_____ Humidity:_____

Weather ☼ ⚡ _____
Moon Phase:_____
Tide Phase:_____
Notes:_____

Species:	Bait:	Length:	Weight:	Time:
Other Notes:				
Other Notes:				
Other Notes:				
Other Notes:				

Fishing Log

Location:_____ Date:_____
Location Details: _____
_____
Companions:_____
Water Temp:_____ Air Temp:_____
Hours Fished:_____ Wind Direction:_____
WInd Speed:_____ Humidity:_____

Weather ☀⚡ _____
Moon Phase:_____
Tide Phase:_____
Notes:_____

Species:	Bait:	Length:	Weight:	Time:
Other Notes:				
Other Notes:				
Other Notes:				
Other Notes:				

Fishing Log

Location:_____ Date:_____
Location Details: _____
_____
Companions:_____
Water Temp:_____ Air Temp:_____
Hours Fished:_____ Wind Direction:_____
WInd Speed:_____ Humidity:_____

Weather ☀️⚡ _____
Moon Phase:_____
Tide Phase:_____
Notes:_____

Species:	Bait:	Length:	Weight:	Time:
Other Notes:				
Other Notes:				
Other Notes:				
Other Notes:				

Fishing Log

Location:_____ Date:_____
Location Details: _____
_____
Companions:_____
Water Temp:_____ Air Temp:_____
Hours Fished:_____ Wind Direction:_____
WInd Speed:_____ Humidity:_____

Weather ☼⚡ _____
Moon Phase:_____
Tide Phase:_____
Notes:_____

Species:	Bait:	Length:	Weight:	Time:

Other Notes:

Other Notes:

Other Notes:

Other Notes:

Fishing Log

Location:_____ Date:_____
Location Details: _____
_____
Companions:_____
Water Temp:_____ Air Temp:_____
Hours Fished:_____ Wind Direction:_____
WInd Speed:_____ Humidity:_____

Weather ☀⚡ _____
Moon Phase:_____
Tide Phase:_____
Notes:_____

Species:	Bait:	Length:	Weight:	Time:
Other Notes:				
Other Notes:				
Other Notes:				
Other Notes:				

Fishing Log

Location:_____ Date:_____
Location Details: _____
_____
Companions:_____
Water Temp:_____ Air Temp:_____
Hours Fished:_____ Wind Direction:_____
Wind Speed:_____ Humidity:_____

Weather ☼⚡_____
Moon Phase:_____
Tide Phase:_____
Notes:_____

Species:	Bait:	Length:	Weight:	Time:

Other Notes:

Other Notes:

Other Notes:

Other Notes:

Fishing Log

Location:_____ Date:_____
Location Details: _____
_____
Companions:_____
Water Temp:_____ Air Temp:_____
Hours Fished:_____ Wind Direction:_____
WInd Speed:_____ Humidity:_____

Weather ☼ ⚡_____
Moon Phase:_____
Tide Phase:_____
Notes:_____

Species:	Bait:	Length:	Weight:	Time:
Other Notes:				
Other Notes:				
Other Notes:				
Other Notes:				

Fishing Log

Location:_____ Date:_____
Location Details: _____
_____
Companions:_____
Water Temp:_____ Air Temp:_____
Hours Fished:_____ Wind Direction:_____
WInd Speed:_____ Humidity:_____

Weather ☀ ⚡ _____
Moon Phase:_____
Tide Phase:_____
Notes:_____

Species:	Bait:	Length:	Weight:	Time:

Other Notes:

Other Notes:

Other Notes:

Other Notes:

Fishing Log

Location:_____ Date:_____
Location Details: _____
_____
Companions:_____
Water Temp:_____ Air Temp:_____
Hours Fished:_____ Wind Direction:_____
WInd Speed:_____ Humidity:_____

Weather ☀ ⚡ _____
Moon Phase:_____
Tide Phase:_____
Notes:_____

Species:	Bait:	Length:	Weight:	Time:
Other Notes:				
Other Notes:				
Other Notes:				
Other Notes:				

Fishing Log

Location:_____ Date:_____
Location Details: _____
_____
Companions:_____
Water Temp:_____ Air Temp:_____
Hours Fished:_____ Wind Direction:_____
WInd Speed:_____ Humidity:_____

Weather ☀️⚡ _____
Moon Phase:_____
Tide Phase:_____
Notes:_____

Species:	Bait:	Length:	Weight:	Time:
Other Notes:				
Other Notes:				
Other Notes:				
Other Notes:				

Fishing Log

Location:_____ Date:_____

Location Details: _____

_____

Companions:_____

Water Temp:_____ Air Temp:_____

Hours Fished:_____ Wind Direction:_____

Wlnd Speed:_____ Humidity:_____

Weather ☀⚡ _____

Moon Phase:_____

Tide Phase:_____

Notes:_____

Species:	Bait:	Length:	Weight:	Time:
Other Notes:				
Other Notes:				
Other Notes:				
Other Notes:				

Fishing Log

Location:_____ Date:_____
Location Details: _____
_____
Companions:_____
Water Temp:_____ Air Temp:_____
Hours Fished:_____ Wind Direction:_____
WInd Speed:_____ Humidity:_____

Weather ☀⚡ _____
Moon Phase:_____
Tide Phase:_____
Notes:_____

Species:	Bait:	Length:	Weight:	Time:

Other Notes:

Other Notes:

Other Notes:

Other Notes:

Fishing Log

Location:_____ Date:_____
Location Details: _____
_____
Companions:_____
Water Temp:_____ Air Temp:_____
Hours Fished:_____ Wind Direction:_____
Wlnd Speed:_____ Humidity:_____

Weather ☀️⚡ _____
Moon Phase:_____
Tide Phase:_____
Notes:_____

Species:	Bait:	Length:	Weight:	Time:
Other Notes:				
Other Notes:				
Other Notes:				
Other Notes:				

Fishing Log

Location:_____ Date:_____
Location Details: _____
_____
Companions:_____
Water Temp:_____ Air Temp:_____
Hours Fished:_____ Wind Direction:_____
WInd Speed:_____ Humidity:_____

Weather ☀⚡_____
Moon Phase:_____
Tide Phase:_____
Notes:_____

Species:	Bait:	Length:	Weight:	Time:

Other Notes:

Other Notes:

Other Notes:

Other Notes:

Fishing Log

Location:_____ Date:_____
Location Details: _____
_____
Companions:_____
Water Temp:_____ Air Temp:_____
Hours Fished:_____ Wind Direction:_____
WInd Speed:_____ Humidity:_____

Weather ☀⚡ _____
Moon Phase:_____
Tide Phase:_____
Notes:_____

Species:	Bait:	Length:	Weight:	Time:
Other Notes:				
Other Notes:				
Other Notes:				
Other Notes:				

Fishing Log

Location:_____ Date:_____
Location Details: _____
_____
Companions:_____
Water Temp:_____ Air Temp:_____
Hours Fished:_____ Wind Direction:_____
WInd Speed:_____ Humidity:_____

Weather ☀⚡ _____
Moon Phase:_____
Tide Phase:_____
Notes:_____

Species:	Bait:	Length:	Weight:	Time:
Other Notes:				
Other Notes:				
Other Notes:				
Other Notes:				

Fishing Log

Location:_____ Date:_____
Location Details: _____
_____
Companions:_____
Water Temp:_____ Air Temp:_____
Hours Fished:_____ Wind Direction:_____
WInd Speed:_____ Humidity:_____

Weather ☼ ⚡ _____
Moon Phase:_____
Tide Phase:_____
Notes:_____

Species:	Bait:	Length:	Weight:	Time:
Other Notes:				
Other Notes:				
Other Notes:				
Other Notes:				

Fishing Log

Location:_____ Date:_____
Location Details: _____
_____
Companions:_____
Water Temp:_____ Air Temp:_____
Hours Fished:_____ Wind Direction:_____
WInd Speed:_____ Humidity:_____

Weather ☀⚡_____
Moon Phase:_____
Tide Phase:_____
Notes:_____

Species:	Bait:	Length:	Weight:	Time:

Other Notes:

Other Notes:

Other Notes:

Other Notes:

Fishing Log

Location:_____ Date:_____
Location Details: _____
_____
Companions:_____
Water Temp:_____ Air Temp:_____
Hours Fished:_____ Wind Direction:_____
WInd Speed:_____ Humidity:_____

Weather ☀ ⚡ _____
Moon Phase:_____
Tide Phase:_____
Notes:_____

Species:	Bait:	Length:	Weight:	Time:
Other Notes:				
Other Notes:				
Other Notes:				
Other Notes:				

Fishing Log

Location:_____ Date:_____
Location Details: _____
_____
Companions:_____
Water Temp:_____ Air Temp:_____
Hours Fished:_____ Wind Direction:_____
WInd Speed:_____ Humidity:_____

Weather ☀⚡ _____
Moon Phase:_____
Tide Phase:_____
Notes:_____

Species:	Bait:	Length:	Weight:	Time:

Other Notes:

Other Notes:

Other Notes:

Other Notes:

Fishing Log

Location:_____ Date:_____
Location Details: _____
_____
Companions:_____
Water Temp:_____ Air Temp:_____
Hours Fished:_____ Wind Direction:_____
WInd Speed:_____ Humidity:_____

Weather ☀⚡ _____
Moon Phase:_____
Tide Phase:_____
Notes:_____

Species:	Bait:	Length:	Weight:	Time:
Other Notes:				
Other Notes:				
Other Notes:				
Other Notes:				

Fishing Log

Location:_____ Date:_____
Location Details: _____
_____
Companions:_____
Water Temp:_____ Air Temp:_____
Hours Fished:_____ Wind Direction:_____
WInd Speed:_____ Humidity:_____

Weather ☀ ⚡ _____
Moon Phase:_____
Tide Phase:_____
Notes:_____

Species:	Bait:	Length:	Weight:	Time:

Other Notes:

Other Notes:

Other Notes:

Other Notes:

Fishing Log

Location:_____ Date:_____
Location Details: _____
_____
Companions:_____
Water Temp:_____ Air Temp:_____
Hours Fished:_____ Wind Direction:_____
WInd Speed:_____ Humidity:_____

Weather ☀⚡ _____
Moon Phase:_____
Tide Phase:_____
Notes:_____

Species:	Bait:	Length:	Weight:	Time:
Other Notes:				
Other Notes:				
Other Notes:				
Other Notes:				

Fishing Log

Location:_____ Date:_____
Location Details: _____
_____
Companions:_____
Water Temp:_____ Air Temp:_____
Hours Fished:_____ Wind Direction:_____
WInd Speed:_____ Humidity:_____

Weather ☀⚡ _____
Moon Phase:_____
Tide Phase:_____
Notes:_____

Species:	Bait:	Length:	Weight:	Time:

Other Notes:

Other Notes:

Other Notes:

Other Notes:

Fishing Log

Location:_____ Date:_____
Location Details: _____
_____
Companions:_____
Water Temp:_____ Air Temp:_____
Hours Fished:_____ Wind Direction:_____
WInd Speed:_____ Humidity:_____

Weather ☼ ⚡ _____
Moon Phase:_____
Tide Phase:_____
Notes:_____

Species:	Bait:	Length:	Weight:	Time:
Other Notes:				
Other Notes:				
Other Notes:				
Other Notes:				

Fishing Log

Location:_____ Date:_____
Location Details: _____
_____
Companions:_____
Water Temp:_____ Air Temp:_____
Hours Fished:_____ Wind Direction:_____
WInd Speed:_____ Humidity:_____

Weather ☀ ⚡ _____
Moon Phase:_____
Tide Phase:_____
Notes:_____

Species:	Bait:	Length:	Weight:	Time:

Other Notes:

Other Notes:

Other Notes:

Other Notes:

Fishing Log

Location:_____ Date:_____
Location Details: _____
_____
Companions:_____
Water Temp:_____ Air Temp:_____
Hours Fished:_____ Wind Direction:_____
WInd Speed:_____ Humidity:_____

Weather ☀️⚡ _____
Moon Phase:_____
Tide Phase:_____
Notes:_____

Species:	Bait:	Length:	Weight:	Time:
Other Notes:				
Other Notes:				
Other Notes:				
Other Notes:				

Fishing Log

Location:_____ Date:_____
Location Details: _____
_____
Companions:_____
Water Temp:_____ Air Temp:_____
Hours Fished:_____ Wind Direction:_____
WInd Speed:_____ Humidity:_____

Weather ☀⚡ _____
Moon Phase:_____
Tide Phase:_____
Notes:_____

Species:	Bait:	Length:	Weight:	Time:

Other Notes:

Other Notes:

Other Notes:

Other Notes:

Fishing Log

Location:_____ Date:_____
Location Details: _____
_____
Companions:_____
Water Temp:_____ Air Temp:_____
Hours Fished:_____ Wind Direction:_____
WInd Speed:_____ Humidity:_____

Weather ☀ ⚡ _____
Moon Phase:_____
Tide Phase:_____
Notes:_____

Species:	Bait:	Length:	Weight:	Time:
Other Notes:				
Other Notes:				
Other Notes:				
Other Notes:				

Fishing Log

Location:_____ Date:_____
Location Details: _____
_____
Companions:_____
Water Temp:_____ Air Temp:_____
Hours Fished:_____ Wind Direction:_____
Wind Speed:_____ Humidity:_____

Weather ☀⚡_____
Moon Phase:_____
Tide Phase:_____
Notes:_____

Species:	Bait:	Length:	Weight:	Time:

Other Notes:

Other Notes:

Other Notes:

Other Notes:

Fishing Log

Location:_____ Date:_____
Location Details: _____
_____
Companions:_____
Water Temp:_____ Air Temp:_____
Hours Fished:_____ Wind Direction:_____
WInd Speed:_____ Humidity:_____

Weather ☀️⚡ _____
Moon Phase:_____
Tide Phase:_____
Notes:_____

Species:	Bait:	Length:	Weight:	Time:
Other Notes:				
Other Notes:				
Other Notes:				
Other Notes:				

Fishing Log

Location:_____ Date:_____
Location Details: _____
_____
Companions:_____
Water Temp:_____ Air Temp:_____
Hours Fished:_____ Wind Direction:_____
WInd Speed:_____ Humidity:_____

Weather ☀⚡ _____
Moon Phase:_____
Tide Phase:_____
Notes:_____

Species:	Bait:	Length:	Weight:	Time:

Other Notes:

Other Notes:

Other Notes:

Other Notes:

Fishing Log

Location:_____ **Date:**_____

Location Details: _____

_____

Companions:_____

Water Temp:_____ **Air Temp:**_____

Hours Fished:_____ **Wind Direction:**_____

WInd Speed:_____ **Humidity:**_____

Weather ☼ ⚡ _____

Moon Phase:_____

Tide Phase:_____

Notes:_____

Species:	Bait:	Length:	Weight:	Time:
Other Notes:				
Other Notes:				
Other Notes:				
Other Notes:				

Fishing Log

Location:_____ Date:_____

Location Details: _____

_____

Companions:_____

Water Temp:_____ Air Temp:_____

Hours Fished:_____ Wind Direction:_____

WInd Speed:_____ Humidity:_____

Weather ☀⚡ _____

Moon Phase:_____

Tide Phase:_____

Notes:_____

Species:	Bait:	Length:	Weight:	Time:

Other Notes:

Other Notes:

Other Notes:

Other Notes:

Fishing Log

Location:_____ Date:_____
Location Details: _____
_____
Companions:_____
Water Temp:_____ Air Temp:_____
Hours Fished:_____ Wind Direction:_____
Wlnd Speed:_____ Humidity:_____

Weather ☀⚡ _____
Moon Phase:_____
Tide Phase:_____
Notes:_____

Species:	Bait:	Length:	Weight:	Time:
Other Notes:				
Other Notes:				
Other Notes:				
Other Notes:				

Fishing Log

Location:_____ Date:_____
Location Details: _____
_____
Companions:_____
Water Temp:_____ Air Temp:_____
Hours Fished:_____ Wind Direction:_____
Wind Speed:_____ Humidity:_____

Weather ☀⚡_____
Moon Phase:_____
Tide Phase:_____
Notes:_____

Species:	Bait:	Length:	Weight:	Time:

Other Notes:

Other Notes:

Other Notes:

Other Notes:

Fishing Log

Location:_____ Date:_____
Location Details: _____
_____
Companions:_____
Water Temp:_____ Air Temp:_____
Hours Fished:_____ Wind Direction:_____
Wlnd Speed:_____ Humidity:_____

Weather ☀⚡ _____
Moon Phase:_____
Tide Phase:_____
Notes:_____

Species:	Bait:	Length:	Weight:	Time:
Other Notes:				
Other Notes:				
Other Notes:				
Other Notes:				

Fishing Log

Location:_____ Date:_____
Location Details: _____
_____
Companions:_____
Water Temp:_____ Air Temp:_____
Hours Fished:_____ Wind Direction:_____
WInd Speed:_____ Humidity:_____

Weather ☼ ⚡ _____
Moon Phase:_____
Tide Phase:_____
Notes:_____

Species:	Bait:	Length:	Weight:	Time:

Other Notes:

Other Notes:

Other Notes:

Other Notes:

Fishing Log

Location:_____ Date:_____
Location Details: _____
_____

Companions:_____
Water Temp:_____ Air Temp:_____
Hours Fished:_____ Wind Direction:_____
WInd Speed:_____ Humidity:_____

Weather ☼ ⚡ _____
Moon Phase:_____
Tide Phase:_____
Notes:_____

Species:	Bait:	Length:	Weight:	Time:
Other Notes:				
Other Notes:				
Other Notes:				
Other Notes:				

Fishing Log

Location:_____ Date:_____
Location Details: _____

_____

Companions:_____
Water Temp:_____ Air Temp:_____
Hours Fished:_____ Wind Direction:_____
WInd Speed:_____ Humidity:_____

Weather ☀ ⚡ _____
Moon Phase:_____
Tide Phase:_____
Notes:_____

Species:	Bait:	Length:	Weight:	Time:

Other Notes:

Other Notes:

Other Notes:

Other Notes:

Fishing Log

Location:_____ Date:_____
Location Details: _____
_____
Companions:_____
Water Temp:_____ Air Temp:_____
Hours Fished:_____ Wind Direction:_____
WInd Speed:_____ Humidity:_____

Weather ☀️⚡ _____
Moon Phase:_____
Tide Phase:_____
Notes:_____

Species:	Bait:	Length:	Weight:	Time:
Other Notes:				
Other Notes:				
Other Notes:				
Other Notes:				

Fishing Log

Location:_____ Date:_____
Location Details: _____
_____
Companions:_____
Water Temp:_____ Air Temp:_____
Hours Fished:_____ Wind Direction:_____
WInd Speed:_____ Humidity:_____

Weather ☀⚡ _____
Moon Phase:_____
Tide Phase:_____
Notes:_____

Species:	Bait:	Length:	Weight:	Time:

Other Notes:

Other Notes:

Other Notes:

Other Notes:

Fishing Log

Location:_____ Date:_____
Location Details: _____
_____
Companions:_____
Water Temp:_____ Air Temp:_____
Hours Fished:_____ Wind Direction:_____
WInd Speed:_____ Humidity:_____

Weather ☼⚡ _____
Moon Phase:_____
Tide Phase:_____
Notes:_____

Species:	Bait:	Length:	Weight:	Time:
Other Notes:				
Other Notes:				
Other Notes:				
Other Notes:				

Fishing Log

Location:_____ Date:_____
Location Details: _____
_____
Companions:_____
Water Temp:_____ Air Temp:_____
Hours Fished:_____ Wind Direction:_____
WInd Speed:_____ Humidity:_____

Weather ☀⚡ _____
Moon Phase:_____
Tide Phase:_____
Notes:_____

Species:	Bait:	Length:	Weight:	Time:

Other Notes:

Other Notes:

Other Notes:

Other Notes:

Fishing Log

Location:_____ Date:_____
Location Details: _____
_____
Companions:_____
Water Temp:_____ Air Temp:_____
Hours Fished:_____ Wind Direction:_____
WInd Speed:_____ Humidity:_____

Weather ☼ ⚡ _____
Moon Phase:_____
Tide Phase:_____
Notes:_____

Species:	Bait:	Length:	Weight:	Time:
Other Notes:				
Other Notes:				
Other Notes:				
Other Notes:				

Fishing Log

Location:_____ Date:_____
Location Details: _____
_____
Companions:_____
Water Temp:_____ Air Temp:_____
Hours Fished:_____ Wind Direction:_____
WInd Speed:_____ Humidity:_____

Weather ☀ ⚡ _____
Moon Phase:_____
Tide Phase:_____
Notes:_____

Species:	Bait:	Length:	Weight:	Time:

Other Notes:

Other Notes:

Other Notes:

Other Notes:

Fishing Log

Location:_____ Date:_____
Location Details: _____
_____
Companions:_____
Water Temp:_____ Air Temp:_____
Hours Fished:_____ Wind Direction:_____
WInd Speed:_____ Humidity:_____

Weather ☀⚡ _____
Moon Phase:_____
Tide Phase:_____
Notes:_____

Species:	Bait:	Length:	Weight:	Time:
Other Notes:				
Other Notes:				
Other Notes:				
Other Notes:				

Fishing Log

Location:_____ Date:_____
Location Details: _____
_____
Companions:_____
Water Temp:_____ Air Temp:_____
Hours Fished:_____ Wind Direction:_____
WInd Speed:_____ Humidity:_____

Weather ☼ ⚡ _____
Moon Phase:_____
Tide Phase:_____
Notes:_____

Species:	Bait:	Length:	Weight:	Time:

Other Notes:

Other Notes:

Other Notes:

Other Notes:

Fishing Log

Location:_____ Date:_____
Location Details: _____
_____
Companions:_____
Water Temp:_____ Air Temp:_____
Hours Fished:_____ Wind Direction:_____
WInd Speed:_____ Humidity:_____

Weather ☀⚡ _____
Moon Phase:_____
Tide Phase:_____
Notes:_____

Species:	Bait:	Length:	Weight:	Time:
Other Notes:				
Other Notes:				
Other Notes:				
Other Notes:				

Fishing Log

Location:_____ Date:_____
Location Details: _____
_____
Companions:_____
Water Temp:_____ Air Temp:_____
Hours Fished:_____ Wind Direction:_____
Wind Speed:_____ Humidity:_____

Weather ☀️⚡ _____
Moon Phase:_____
Tide Phase:_____
Notes:_____

Species:	Bait:	Length:	Weight:	Time:

Other Notes:

Other Notes:

Other Notes:

Other Notes:

Fishing Log

Location:_____ Date:_____
Location Details: _____
_____
Companions:_____
Water Temp:_____ Air Temp:_____
Hours Fished:_____ Wind Direction:_____
Wind Speed:_____ Humidity:_____

Weather ☀️⚡ _____
Moon Phase:_____
Tide Phase:_____
Notes:_____

Species:	Bait:	Length:	Weight:	Time:
Other Notes:				
Other Notes:				
Other Notes:				
Other Notes:				

Fishing Log

Location:_____ Date:_____
Location Details: _____
_____
Companions:_____
Water Temp:_____ Air Temp:_____
Hours Fished:_____ Wind Direction:_____
Wind Speed:_____ Humidity:_____

Weather ☀⚡ _____
Moon Phase:_____
Tide Phase:_____
Notes:_____

Species:	Bait:	Length:	Weight:	Time:

Other Notes:

Other Notes:

Other Notes:

Other Notes:

Fishing Log

Location:_____ Date:_____
Location Details: _____
_____
Companions:_____
Water Temp:_____ Air Temp:_____
Hours Fished:_____ Wind Direction:_____
WInd Speed:_____ Humidity:_____

Weather ☀⚡ _____
Moon Phase:_____
Tide Phase:_____
Notes:_____

Species:	Bait:	Length:	Weight:	Time:
Other Notes:				
Other Notes:				
Other Notes:				
Other Notes:				

Fishing Log

Location:_____ Date:_____
Location Details: _____
_____
Companions:_____
Water Temp:_____ Air Temp:_____
Hours Fished:_____ Wind Direction:_____
WInd Speed:_____ Humidity:_____

Weather ☀ ⚡ _____
Moon Phase:_____
Tide Phase:_____
Notes:_____

Species:	Bait:	Length:	Weight:	Time:

Other Notes:

Other Notes:

Other Notes:

Other Notes:

Fishing Log

Location:_____ Date:_____
Location Details: _____
_____
Companions:_____
Water Temp:_____ Air Temp:_____
Hours Fished:_____ Wind Direction:_____
WInd Speed:_____ Humidity:_____

Weather ☀⚡_____
Moon Phase:_____
Tide Phase:_____
Notes:_____

Species:	Bait:	Length:	Weight:	Time:
Other Notes:				
Other Notes:				
Other Notes:				
Other Notes:				

Fishing Log

Location:_____ Date:_____
Location Details: _____
_____
Companions:_____
Water Temp:_____ Air Temp:_____
Hours Fished:_____ Wind Direction:_____
Wind Speed:_____ Humidity:_____

Weather ☼ ⚡ _____
Moon Phase:_____
Tide Phase:_____
Notes:_____

Species:	Bait:	Length:	Weight:	Time:

Other Notes:

Other Notes:

Other Notes:

Other Notes:

Fishing Log

Location:_____ Date:_____
Location Details: _____
_____
Companions:_____
Water Temp:_____ Air Temp:_____
Hours Fished:_____ Wind Direction:_____
WInd Speed:_____ Humidity:_____

Weather ☀⚡ _____
Moon Phase:_____
Tide Phase:_____
Notes:_____

Species:	Bait:	Length:	Weight:	Time:
Other Notes:				
Other Notes:				
Other Notes:				
Other Notes:				

Fishing Log

Location:_____ Date:_____
Location Details: _____
_____
Companions:_____
Water Temp:_____ Air Temp:_____
Hours Fished:_____ Wind Direction:_____
Wind Speed:_____ Humidity:_____

Weather ☀ ⚡ _____
Moon Phase:_____
Tide Phase:_____
Notes:_____

Species:	Bait:	Length:	Weight:	Time:

Other Notes:

Other Notes:

Other Notes:

Other Notes:

Fishing Log

Location:_____ **Date:**_____
Location Details: _____
_____
Companions:_____
Water Temp:_____ **Air Temp:**_____
Hours Fished:_____ **Wind Direction:**_____
WInd Speed:_____ **Humidity:**_____

Weather ☼ ⚡ _____
Moon Phase:_____
Tide Phase:_____
Notes:_____

Species:	Bait:	Length:	Weight:	Time:
Other Notes:				
Other Notes:				
Other Notes:				
Other Notes:				

Fishing Log

Location:_____ Date:_____
Location Details: _____
_____
Companions:_____
Water Temp:_____ Air Temp:_____
Hours Fished:_____ Wind Direction:_____
WInd Speed:_____ Humidity:_____

Weather ☀ ⚡ _____
Moon Phase:_____
Tide Phase:_____
Notes:_____

Species:	Bait:	Length:	Weight:	Time:

Other Notes:

Other Notes:

Other Notes:

Other Notes:

Fishing Log

Location:_____ Date:_____
Location Details: _____
_____
Companions:_____
Water Temp:_____ Air Temp:_____
Hours Fished:_____ Wind Direction:_____
WInd Speed:_____ Humidity:_____

Weather ☀⚡ _____
Moon Phase:_____
Tide Phase:_____
Notes:_____

Species:	Bait:	Length:	Weight:	Time:
Other Notes:				
Other Notes:				
Other Notes:				
Other Notes:				

Fishing Log

Location:_____ Date:_____
Location Details: _____
_____
Companions:_____
Water Temp:_____ Air Temp:_____
Hours Fished:_____ Wind Direction:_____
WInd Speed:_____ Humidity:_____

Weather ☼ ⚡ _____
Moon Phase:_____
Tide Phase:_____
Notes:_____

Species:	Bait:	Length:	Weight:	Time:

Other Notes:

Other Notes:

Other Notes:

Other Notes:

Fishing Log

Location:_____ Date:_____
Location Details: _____
_____
Companions:_____
Water Temp:_____ Air Temp:_____
Hours Fished:_____ Wind Direction:_____
WInd Speed:_____ Humidity:_____

Weather ☀⚡ _____
Moon Phase:_____
Tide Phase:_____
Notes:_____

Species:	Bait:	Length:	Weight:	Time:
Other Notes:				
Other Notes:				
Other Notes:				
Other Notes:				

Printed in Great Britain
by Amazon